THE LIVE ALBUM

Payne Ware

ISBN: 978-1-913642-56-3

Book designed by Aaron Kent

Edited by Aaron Kent

Broken Sleep Books (2021), Talgarreg, Wales

TRACKS

SIDE A: "CUTS"

SIDE B: "PRODUCTION"

'The animals in THE LIVE ALBUM may be slaughtered, but they are not dead. Always confronting and often striking in their subtle tragicomedy, Kat Payne Ware's poems find astonishing voice in these cuts of meat that in turn cut away at our conventions of consumption. This is a rare and powerful poetics of nonhuman intimacy.'

- ***Isabel Galleymore***

'In THE LIVE ALBUM Kat Payne Ware attains an intensity of observation and analysis that marks out the best poetry. Meticulously crafted images and porcine voices take us from the plate back to the slaughterhouse. In one sense it's a book about displacement, and one that forces us to look clearly at something we'd rather keep hidden, with a formal innovation that matches the horrifying technologies explored. But instead of a polemic we encounter something lyrical, soulful and frequently moving. A shockingly good collection and an infinitely promising debut.'

- ***Luke Kennard***

'The literature of meat has too long been confined to realist novels and recipe books. Kat Payne Ware's THE LIVE ALBUM changes all that, with laser-sharp lyrics in an acrobatic array of forms that put the whole pig-eating industry on display. By turns fascinating and chilling, the acute playfulness of this poetry is a function of its empathy: a deep-dive documentary into carnivorous modernity that subjects the inhuman to unexpected enjambments, metaphors and emotions, 'running arrhyhmic desire lines through the hearty text of me.'

- ***Jeremy Noel-Tod***

THE LIVE ALBUM

Kat Payne Ware

And the pigs — hushed, breathing
calmly in their pens — quiet us into handlers.

Jenny George, 'Influence'

SIDE A

"CUTS"

BACON

To work backwards, I leave
the tongue's wet airstrip.
I travel in reverse with the scalic
whirr of a rewinding
VHS cassette as the fork
takes a taildive back to the plate.
I touchdown in a pool of ketchup
and the opposite of stabbing happens.
The tape speeds up: baked beans
levitate forming a mob in the air
as they are drawn to the lip
of the pan like iron filings
and the toast regurgitates its butter
back onto the hovering knife.
Eventually the tongs arrive
and I am out of the fire
and into the frying pan, buckling
like a red wave before falling
limp and shedding a gradation
of colour. A mammoth
finger and thumb descend
and return me to the packet
where I struggle to find
an antonym for peeling off
from my traymates. Perhaps I cover
them? Perhaps they put me on?

SAUSAGES

meaning salted: Vulgar
Latin *salsicus*. Meaning
reformed. Meaning second
chance. To be ground

is to be returned to basics.
Now I matter.
To be stretched
further with meal

and water is to account
for the scant of I.
Is to grow from ground
overnight as magic

beans. Now I *banger*:
explode myself
from myself as skin
shrinks upon introduction

of masticating heat.
Bursting seams
imagine I as Jupiter, granting
two second chances

to a ridiculous man.
Imagine this man's wife
becoming sausageless
and wanting.

Isn't this the way
it always was? I
inside of I, nesting
Tupperware, I twisted

like farfalle, like pipe
cleaner. In any case
I crocodile feed
as Punch's face thumbs
                                        apart

CHEEK

a versatile, flavoursome and cheap cut that deserves much more attention
- Campbells Prime Meat Ltd., *A-Z of Meat*

Tell me am I worthy
am I deserving
of attention. Am I a wet
chunk of versatility.
Call me *guanciale*
when we pillow talk.
Let me turn the other
for a little kiss.
O to be underrated
to shy from praise
and to bruise slow
in cheap cider
and a low heat.
O to sit in the basin
of the cheek below
the eyes. Silent!
I fall apart at the touch
of a fork. Tenderise
me, treat me like a bad
good dog. Give me
what I deserve
tell me am I worthy.

RIBS

Carve me as a figurehead, baby.
Acknowledge those without whose support
you would not have been able to produce
such a fine work. I've got a primal
quality, they'll agree, in the vein
of something Hirst might exhibit.

Be aware that gallery visitors may exhibit
some signs of distress. A baby
is likely to slice through the vein
of silence in instinctive support
of animal things. This is primal
and cannot be avoided except by producing

something to chew on: local produce
is best. I'll stay quiet as an exhibit
should, and attempt to contain primal
leakage as far as possible, baby.
In the foyer a violin might sing, supported
by the hum of the blood in your jugular vein.

One critic likens my structure to the vein
of a leaf or a ship's timber, producing
an altogether new interpretation supported
by a majority of the exhibit's
audience. At home are his wife and baby
and a spitting joint in his primal

oven, taken from the animal's primal
cut. The critic fancies himself in the vein
of Adam, believing his wife was never a baby
but was born from his own produce.
The cage of his umbrella exhibits
a show of grand support.

I'd like to thank those without whose support
I would have never have escaped my primal
function. Thanks to you whose carving exhibited
such skill. In geology a rib is a vein
therefore an unsuspecting rock can produce
a rib of gold like a valuable baby.

The proceeds of this exhibit will go towards the support
of my carver's new baby, who I can honestly say is a prime
example, from bone to vein, of the best local produce.

BELLY

I am squat in geometric regularity candy striped
the colours of red gingham read my layers like
the layers of the earth topsoil of pearly magnolia
its diameter whispering *well fed* or *force fed runt*
or *prize* then in gentle white and blush a marbling
effect most desirable on countertops fat running
arrhythmic desire lines through the hearty text
of me the tender pink of me before the final claret
third like the last beat of sashimi like crustaceans
shifting in saran wrap like the fractals of a grapefruit
bellyaching by the boiled egg o slippery uncut ruby
dark around organs in its high security home now
musselfoot suckered to the plastic tray now I am
a die and all my six terrible faces lucky lucky sixes

SCRATCHINGS

You ask her why she is wearing gloves
in summer. She tells you she has ugly
hands and is afraid to bare them.
In actual fact her hands are beautiful.
She used to say to strangers
she was scouted as a hand model
in a local mall, but this was a lie.
Nobody has ever noticed or
commented upon her beautiful hands.
The fingers are long and the nails are long
by which she doesn't mean unclipped
but bedded high on the finger and so
having the appearance of slenderness.
The ratio of finger to palm is fair
(probably fifty-fifty) and she keeps
the backs well moisturised. These are not
men's hands by which she means
labourers', and she fancies them the mark
of an elegant eighteenth-century life.
In actual fact she is wearing the gloves
not to cover the hands but to temper
their aptitude for exceptional violence.
Through the introduction of soft barriers
(felts, fur linings) she hopes to dissuade
them from attacking other parts
of her body. You haven't asked why
she covers her legs and the accessible area
of her back, and have made no mention
of the balaclava. The truth is that
if you were to remove these layers
she would be sorely missing
various essential pieces.

BLOOD

Blood is associated not with true life, but with its pale and ghostly counterpart.
- Dennis J. McCarthy, 'The Symbolism of Blood and Sacrifice'

I spin my red wool
in the purificatory rite
of a spider dropping
stitches onto steel
altars. My *šurpu* lifts
all kinds of curses
and bodily pains.
Let me sing for you
a red song. Let my
shedding raise the
"strengthless dead"
in supplication
that you and they
may confer. Do you
wish to change
your answer. Pet
food and a half
life of millennia, or
Circe's punishment.
Is it better to be blood
or swine. Consider
that when I am spilt
on infertile land
I spring immediately
into gold, ripe corn.

SHOULDER

the most forgiving cut on the animal
- Kevin Gillespie, *Pure Pork Awesomeness*

The theatrics of forgiveness
are fairly simple to master.

On the internet you can read about
Ten Great Moments in Forgiveness History.

The shortlist includes Jesus Christ
Nelson Mandela and Genghis Khan.

A decision has been made to order
the moments chronologically and as such

we are not given a number one.
The penultimate case is from 2003

or just shy of two millennia
from Jesus' commended act:

In a dramatic event captured on CBS
Reo Hatfield and Bo McCoy sign an "official truce"

that formally ends a more than century-old
family feud that began over a stolen pig.

The pig was not interviewed
but there were several sightings

and one enthusiast has gained
a large following for his theory

based on a grainy pink face, spotted
for an instant to the left of Hatfield's shoulder

in the background of the CBS recording.

FILLET

I hang from the tongs like a long pink tongue. A tongue only lolls when the animal is panting or dead. Put me down on the tray. Dream some Frankensteinian science brings me round with the urgent throe of defibrillation. I begin to creep across the counter in the peristaltic motion of legless things. My direction of movement makes head and tail of me — to have direction one cannot just be meat. I concertina, accordionlike, edge toward the knife-edge, then rear into an S like a weasel. My blunt end is levelled with your face. Neither of us can speak. Then, in this dream, I find your mouth, quick kiss, then enter and worm down your gullet. I traverse your inner systems. In this dream, your gullet is a wormhole: I emerge having pilgrimaged to a new place. This kitchen is populated by long pink tongues. On the tray lies something with legs.

LOIN

And we were hoping for a high yield
and we prayed to the pGH for a high yield.

I dome from the dish in the echo of a polytunnel
my rotunda bouncing echoes of a cry: *yield*.

I'm like the story of loaves and fishes:
we've built a church from grains. Why yield

now? Why not lift the crackling roof
like a stone and let the light in? I yield

to the blade, peel away from myself in a gentle
ballroom dip — this trust exercise might yield

a knowledge of strong arches. Circular structures
are a nightmare to construct but nice on the eye. Yield

to my curvature: no Greeks carved vertices.
Imagine me, Loin, a product of the sty.

Side B

“PRODUCTION”

CURING

[redacted] is [redacted]
easy to do at home.
It works by [redacted]
killing [redacted]
creating an enhanced "umami" taste
we will revisit [redacted]
the flesh
more tender.
Cured meats are [redacted]
meat's red colour. [redacted]
but [redacted]
curing your own
meat [redacted] may end up
an unattractive grey [redacted]
on the other hand — [redacted]
the Swedish word
for grave [redacted] might be described as
challenging: [redacted]
one of the worst things [redacted]
however,
[redacted] is only lightly cured. This is enough to extend its [redacted]
life by a few days, but not weeks.

Start with [redacted]
bones [redacted] coarse [redacted]
ground [redacted] works well.
Rub the [redacted]
skin [redacted] down. [redacted]
Keep [redacted] for a day, then [redacted]

[redacted] cut some slices and [redacted]

bury them [redacted]

BUTCHERING

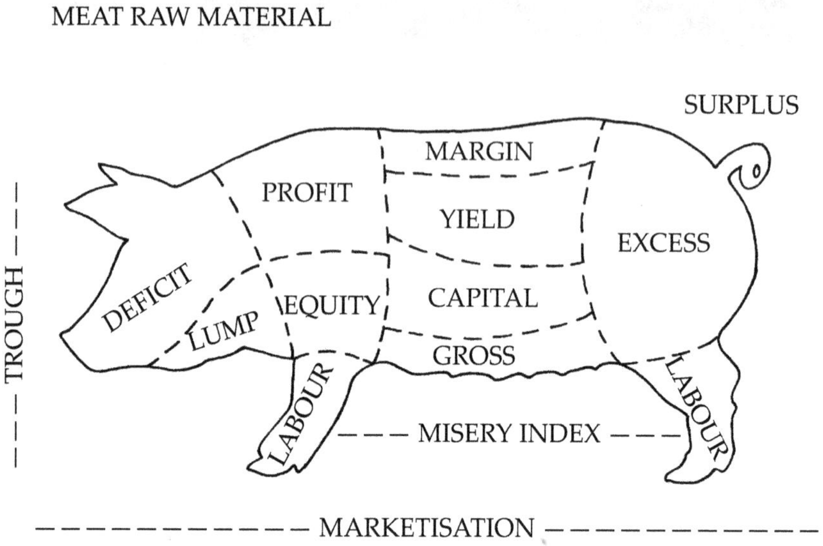

MEAT RAW MATERIAL
SURPLUS
MARGIN
PROFIT
YIELD
EXCESS
DEFICIT
LUMP
EQUITY
CAPITAL
GROSS
LABOUR
LABOUR
MISERY INDEX
TROUGH
MARKETISATION

PRINTING

It's all plug and play — print a picture if you want
and up to three lines of text on every primal cut.

Automatically process each carcass by the individual
length. Printing of a health mark is possible.

Performance of homogeneous processing: fixation
belts secure and support us all the way. Easy operation

uniform user-friendly operator panel and trouble-
shooting. Pull us forward by drop fingers, double

sided, synchronised. This is a dynamic concept: even
and clear print result with flexible heads. Cleaning

easy and efficient. High capacity. High
quality carcasses with fixation. Designed

in accordance with the EU and USDA regulations
to meet the strictest demand on health. Fixation

and processing can be performed. All's fair
in plug and play. 750-1,200 carcasses/hour.

SPLITTING

And O, thou shalt come before   thy God, and prostrate thyself
before His eye, and, great or small,   thou shalt know thyself measured
by Him. And the red bead of His rosary   will travel thee, and in this He will know
head from trotter, and in this He will know   thee. Thus with Angelic fanfare His cage will
open and thou shalt be conveyed to Him, and   He will move in thee, and in this thou shalt know
His love. And He will split thee into two faces, and open the book of thee, and He will read what is
written in the book, and shall cast the halves   of thee Heavenward or into the lake of fire. And
both Heaven and the lake of fire shall   look the same. And both Heaven and the
lake of fire shall yield thy loin   successfully. And His cage will close
around Him, for He hath   ended His work. And O, from
His presence earth   and sky shall flee away.

FINNING

process is potential
Haarslev Processing Technology

1. Prior to entering the automated zone, the length of the pig is determined by an infrared light curtain.[1]

2. Before processing the pubic bone is measured.[2]

3. Transfer of measurement data takes place from measuring stations, ensuring the tools are set at the correct starting position.[3]

4. To ensure uniform processing, the pig is fixed in the machine by insertion of a pubic guide.[4]

5. A hydraulic circular knife cuts through rind, fat, and, if required, belly and neck.[5]

---

1 *fin*, v. To swim, as a fish; hence used of underwater swimmers.

2 Might you imagine me jackknifed
into deep waters. Finning
camouflaged against the corals, snapped
at by little crabs. Breath escaping
spherified and destined for the skin
of the water like fat in a hot broth.

3 Imagine it: my cumbersome body
lithe in the ocean. Kicking
stubborn legs in a perfect butterfly.
Like a duck to water, like a baby
turning gracefully in the amniotic sac.
Like a single synchronised swimmer.

4 If you had a little jet ski I'd leap
on it. Imagine you and I circling
Big Major Cay in our sexy swimwear
and our waxed skins. The horizon
stretched to the tearing of its ligaments
the water turning to swine.

5 Or: *fin*, v. To cut off the fins from (a fish).

6. Two parallel cutting knives are inserted between vertebra 1 and vertebra 2 and on each side of them. The knives are inserted to a depth corresponding to the bottom of the spinous processes. After insertion the knives follow the spine in a downward movement. This way the spinous processes are back-finned separating bone and meat.[6]

7. The machine has now completed the back finning process from tail to neck and the pig is discharged on the same carrier of the dressing line conveyor as before the process.[7]

6 The Pacific turns red in the wake
of a finning boat. Viewed
from above it looks a lot like a hurricane
warning. Below the boat
the sharks are circling downward as if a plug
has been pulled on the ocean floor.

7 The process is perennial as a wedding
band. So, instead, imagine
us on our jet ski. Imagine me riding up front
you reaching round
your hands on the gears and throttle.
Imagine writing the wake.

EVISCERATION

Emptied like a crate NOTHING NOTHING NOTHING NOTHING of bad oranges.
With my edges un- NOTHING NOTHING NOTHING NOTHING -knitted I am so brand
new and empty NOTHING NOTHING NOTHING NOTHING as bubble wrap. As
a bad wormed apple NOTHING NOTHING NOTHING NOTHING through which the sun
light pokes while NOTHING NOTHING NOTHING NOTHING it still dangles red
on the branch. Am I NOTHING NOTHING NOTHING NOTHING light now. I feel deep
cleaned in a beautiful NOTHING NOTHING NOTHING NOTHING way. My excreta
is a memory of me NOTHING NOTHING NOTHING NOTHING ever having lived
and eaten do you hold NOTHING NOTHING NOTHING NOTHING it in your hands. Is it
warm. Did I ever tell NOTHING NOTHING NOTHING NOTHING you that I once broke
free and ate a black- NOTHING NOTHING NOTHING NOTHING -berry. Wiggled out
the farrowing crate NOTHING NOTHING NOTHING NOTHING at feeding time
and through the open NOTHING NOTHING NOTHING NOTHING door. They found me
a sow's length from NOTHING NOTHING NOTHING NOTHING the shed in a bramble
patch in heavy NOTHING NOTHING NOTHING NOTHING moonlight. Chops
stained and baby NOTHING NOTHING NOTHING NOTHING belly filled to break-
-ing. Is there any NOTHING NOTHING NOTHING NOTHING trace of that. Tell
me am I NOTHING NOTHING NOTHING NOTHING purple inside.

SCALDING

When I'm ready, I'm submerged
and the priestly hands of the hoist
guide me through the long trough
like a platelet though a metal vein. [7]

(On the other end I might expect
to be ejected from a height into
a blue tiled pool, had I been born
with two legs and a white fence.)

Instead I am efficiently unshackled
into the machine where I turn slowly
in a farcical pirouette.[8] During
the process I become reflective

as a buffed nail, as a waxed
bikini line, as a waxing moon.[9]

---

7 Frontmatec recommends positioning the scalding line after the pre-washing machine. Pigs are transported on an overhead conveyor into the scalding line. Frontmatec recommends positioning the scalding line as close as possible to the bristle remover to prevent scalded pigs from being cooled down just before bristles are to be removed. Frontmatec recommends a combination of the scalding line with a Duoplan conveyor and a standard bleeding shackle.

8 From the scalding line, the pigs are automatically un-shackled directly into the Frontmatec dehairing machine designed for lengthwise, continuous introduction and dehairing of pigs. The internal construction with smooth surfaces (rollers with closed ends, insulated, stainless steel side doors, pneumatically operated by means of an open/close button) limits the chance of accumulated dirt and gives easy access for cleaning. This results in improved hygiene levels and waste minimisation – in the end, improving meat quality. In case of a new installation, the machine will traditionally be installed as a double dehairing machine with opposite rotation of each pig, thus achieving the most ideal dehairing process. The dehairing machine is supplied with a primary and a secondary scraper shaft with bolt-on scrapers. During scraping, the hogs rotate forward due to the designs of the supporting lattice (U-bar) and the spiral-shaped drum. The U-bar design and the positioning of the scraper shafts ensure efficient cleaning of both pigs and sows.

9 *How to keep your dehairing machine in an excellent and efficient shape* *Secure continuous high performance* by having your certified Frontmatec service specialist perform a scheduled bearing service, which includes check of bearing leakage and optimal greasing for highest possible protection of the bearings. The trained eyes of your Frontmatec service technician will assess whether the bearing balls still have the right clearance and furthermore secure a smooth operation by carrying out a function test of the deshacklers. *Be prepared for the unexpected* by stocking rubber fenders, drum bearings and paddles. *Lower the operation costs* by prolonging the life-time of your bearings by choosing specifically engineered greases from Frontmatec.

EXSANGUINATION

Torrential would be the word
they'd use on the news, if this
was news. Who'd have thought
the old man to have so much
love in him? He swings me
by the ankles like a happy toddler
who begs for it time and again
whose mother is busy in another
room and not there to say *Put*
her down, honey, she'll smack
her head on something
and then you'll be sorry.
Won't you be sorry? He fixes
me up with my feet on the rail
in a monkeybar dangle, slides
a blade into my carotid artery
and with this, as if his sticking
were a blessing and I Lazarus
my heart begins to beat again.
This part is crucial. Its beating
disciplines the blood into action.

STUNNING

Dear Benjamin,[10] you must have known
I longed to see the stars.[11]

Your lifework brought the current
opportunity within

reach of my skull. Hold it: feel
its weight in your dead hand

notice its play on the right
to bear arms.[12] To bear witness

to the state of things. I'm seized
by a live resistance

as we look to the end together:
this is intimate.

Tell me, Benjamin, what was
it like. To go sober

and sensate in your soiled nightclothes.
Do we say *humane*

or just *human*. You gave to me
an alternating current:

---

10 Sir Benjamin Ward Richardson (1828-1896) was a physician and anaesthetist. He also developed the first "humane" methods of slaughter for livestock animals, before which animals were poleaxed or struck while fully conscious.

11 Stephen Luduc discovered in 1902 that electronarcosis produced a narcotic-like state in animals, and eventually tried it on himself, finding he remained conscious but unable to move, in a dreamlike state similar to sleep paralysis.

12 Non-electronarcotic stunning is most commonly achieved with the captive bolt pistol, a device shaped like a handgun which releases then retracts a penetrating or non-penetrating bolt, striking the forehead and inducing unconsciousness.

two hundred volts and fifteen hundred
Hertz to be stupefied.[13]

Is it time. Will I go gently
or thrashing like a fish

caught out by a bad worm. Might
the Council[14] be assembled

at the end of a long barrel
and a captive audience.

Punch me a third eye: let me
know the universe.

---

13 Modern electronarcosis is performed by applying 200 Volts of high-frequency alternating current of 1500 Hertz for 3 seconds to the temples. Over-stunning adversely affects meat quality, and therefore under-stunning is common.

14 The Council of Justice to Animals (later the Humane Slaughter Association) was established in 1911 to improve the slaughter of livestock and unwanted pets. In the early 1920s, the HSA introduced the first mechanical stunner.

TRANSPORTATION

The fragility, juiciness, desirability and proper taste and smell of meat are the most important qualities of pork for the consumer.
- Urszula Ostaszewska, 'The impact of transport on the quality of pig meat'

DARK, FIRM, DRY,[15] and nose to rump
we convoy cleanly in at twenty-five
degrees. It's dim — the dawn is not yet plump;
our driver carries sleep-fat in his eyes.

The trailer's drainage bed is dark and dry
my footing's firm the first time in a life.
The mister sweats for me, and I recline
happyish, all thought and meat, then light

drives us into day. The boars afright:
the slatted beams flash over us like bar-
codes; a pig is crushed against the night
life's end; the searching torches of the star

transform us in our sunbed. Make us dark.
The day stretched over us like Formica.

---

15 'DFD (dark, firm, dry) meat is characterised by a pH higher than normal. This type of meat occurs when animals are subjected to prolonged stress or intense physical effort immediately prior to slaughter ...
The pig production cycle usually takes place in enclosed buildings, so reducing exposure to sunlight reduces the level of stress'

PALE, SOFT, EXUDATIVE:[16] I'm raw
material. Susceptible enzyme.
O ensemble of cuts, let no flaw
interfere in the production line

let my yield have body. Is it mine –
this walking assemblage, this brass band
of shaking pinkness? Is it nearly time
to snuff my name and let the flaming brand

sing from these wax chops? Businessman
don't be soft. Your part is to exude
confidence. To lead me up the ramp
with pale hands. I need you to delude

me into faith: staring down the bolt
gun, the bolted sow, the bolted door.

---

16 'PSE (pale, soft, exudative) meat is characterised by a faster than usual decrease in pH below 5. This is due to the intense, brief stress response to which animals are exposed immediately prior to slaughter (inappropriate handling of animals during unloading, mixing of unknown individuals).'

NOTES

SAUSAGES references a fairy tale published by Charles Perrault in 1697. In the tale, Jupiter grants a woodcutter three wishes. The woodcutter wishes for sausages. His wife condemns his wasting a wish, and so, enraged, he wishes the sausages attached to her nose. The final wish is used to remove the sausages from her nose, leaving them both no better off than before (except for the sausages...)

The epigraph to CHEEK is from an *A-Z of Meat* written by Campbells Prime Meat Ltd., and the poem quotes and misquotes this text

The epigraph to BLOOD is from an essay by Dennis J. McCarthy, and the poem references ancient beliefs and ritual practices described by McCarthy, also quoting Homer's *The Odyssey,* books x-xi

The epigraph to SHOULDER is from a book by Kevin Gillespie, and the poem quotes a list published by *In Character*

LOIN references the use of pGH, or porcine growth hormone. 'In growing pigs, maximally effective doses of pGH increase average daily gain as much as 10% to 20%, improve feed efficiency 15% to 30%, decrease adipose tissue mass and lipid accretion rates by as much as 50% to 80%, and concurrently increase protein deposition by 50%. These effects are associated with a decrease in feed intake of approximately 10% to 15%,' says Terry D. Etherton

CURING is an erasure of the article 'How to cure everything' by Sam Wong

PRINTING is constructed from text drawn from promotional material for the Frontmatec Autoline Inkjet Stamper API8

SPLITTING misquotes Revelation 20:11-15 and its form pastiches that of George Herbert's 'Easter Wings'. The poem responds to the following passage from Arnon Grunberg's essay, 'Slaughterhouse': 'The only thing a robot is used for is cutting the pig in two. The robot is in a cage, for safety reasons: because the robot sees no difference between pigs and humans, it will cut in half anything that appears before its laser-controlled 'eye'. The robot's movements seem awfully human. I feel a bit sorry for the robot, having to work in a cage like that.'

The epigraph to FINNING is the slogan of Haarslev Processing Technology, and the main body of the text is reprinted from a description of the working process of Haarslev's back finner

The footnotes in SCALDING are taken from the online catalogues for Frontmatec's scalding tank and dehairing machine

The epigraph and footnotes in TRANSPORTATION are taken from an article by Urszula Ostaszewska. The first sonnet quotes A.L. Kennedy, who considers the body as 'a strange balance of thought and meat'

full citations in bibliography

THANKS

are due to the editors of *Seiren*, in whose virtual pages BELLY and PRINTING first appeared, to Chrissy Williams at *PERVERSE*, for selecting BUTCHERING, and to Andrew Cowan at newwriting.net, where BLOOD and LOIN were published last year.

also to Sophie Robinson, Jeremy Noel-Tod, Vahni Capildeo, Rebecca Goss, and Meryl Pugh for their insights on the manuscript, and to Luke Kennard and Isabel Galleymore for their belief in my writing.

to Amanda, Becky, Memoona, Molly, and Sharon, who shared their valuable opinions on many of these poems in our MA workshop group at the University of East Anglia.

to the staff and volunteers at Dean Farm Trust animal sanctuary in Chepstow, particularly those who gave up their time for an interview: Holly, Leo, Marcel, Pete, Sam, and Mary.

to Aaron Kent and the whole team at Broken Sleep for tirelessly championing the books they publish, and for taking a chance on this one.

and to my parents, my friends, and Connor, for their patience and their love.

BIBLIOGRAPHY

Campbells Prime Meat Ltd., *A-Z of Meat* (online) <campbellsmeat.com/inspiration/a-z-of-meat>

Carroll, Robert, and Prickett, Stephen, ed., *The Bible: Authorized King James Version* (Oxford: Oxford World's Classics, 2008)

Etherton, Terry D., 'Porcine Growth Hormone: A Central Metabolic Hormone Involved in the Regulation of Adipose Tissue Growth' in *Nutrition*, vol. 17 no. 10 (Amsterdam: Elsevier, 2001)

Feuerhelm, Brad, and Kennedy, A. L., 'Ordinary Light' in *Granta* vol 120, 'Medicine' (London: Granta Publications, 2012) (viewed online)

Frontmatec, 'Autoline inkjet stamper API8' (online) < frontmatec.com/media/4019/frontmatec-autoline-inkjet-stamper-api8_en.pdf>

Frontmatec, 'Scalding tank', 'Dehairing machine', and 'How to keep your dehairing machine in an excellent and efficient shape' (online) <frontmatec.com/en/pork-solutions/unclean-line/scalding-dehairing>

George, Jenny, *The Dream of Reason* (Port Townsend: Copper Canyon Press, 2018)

Gillespie, Kevin, *Pure Pork Awesomeness* (Kansas City: Andrews McMeel Publishing, 2015)

Grunberg, Arnon, tr. Garrett, Sam, 'Slaughterhouse' in *Granta* vol. 142, 'Animalia'(London: Granta Publications, 2018), pp. 75-95.

Haarslev Processing Technology, 'Back finning and cutting along spine machine' (online) <yumpu.com/en/document/read/35523380/back-finning-and-cutting-along-spine-machine-haarslev-uk-ltd>

Herbert, George, 'Easter Wings' in *The Temple* (Menston: Scolar P., 1968), p. 35

Homer, trans. Palmer, George Herbert, *The Odyssey* (Mineola: Dover Thrift Editions, 1999)

McCarthy, Dennis J., 'The Symbolism of Blood and Sacrifice' in *Journal of Biblical Literature* Vol. 88, No. 2 (Atlanta: The Society of Biblical Literature, 1969), pp. 166-176

Ostaszewska, Urszula, 'The impact of transport on the quality of pig meat' in *World Scientific News* (online) <worldscientificnews.com/wp-content/uploads/2017/05/WSN-78-2017-20-27.pdf>

Perrault, Charles, tr. Philip, Neil, and Simborowski, Nicoletta, 'The Foolish Wishes' in *The Complete Fairy Tales of Charles Perrault* (New York: Clarion Books, 1993), p. 150

Wong, Sam, 'How to cure everything' in *New Scientist*, issue 3267 (1 Feb 2020), p. 51.

Author unknown, 'Ten Great Moments in Forgiveness History' on *In Character* (online, pub. 09/01/08) <incharacter.org/archives/forgiveness/ten-great-moments-in-forgiveness-history>

LAY OUT YOUR UNREST

BONUS TRACK

The first to arrive was a packaging lorry. It ached round the corner with the effort of a large, overfed animal, and eased itself onto the straight. When it reached the gates, it let itself down with a huff, and the driver stepped out to show his papers to the person at the kiosk. I assumed there was a person; it may well have been a robot, as the kiosk was windowless on its road-facing side.

We'd been waiting ten minutes or so on the grassy verge. The grass was dewy in the early morning way, and I toed it. Looking at my feet, I realised my shoes were leather: an old pair, bought in the days when such things didn't matter. I hoped nobody else noticed them.

To my left, a group of women and one man sat or sprawled on the verge, oblivious to the damp. They conversed with quiet enthusiasm about something or other. To my right, a man in a fleece greeted two newcomers in a camp, theatrical voice, sucking hungrily on a vape between introductions. He forgot their names repeatedly, asking,

'And — sorry — your name was? And yours?,' jabbing a genial finger at each in turn.

Unwisely, I was wearing shorts, and the hairs on my legs stood out like cactus spines.

The air stiffened as a car pulled round the corner. The car, a black Porsche, cruised easily to the gates, its driver stepping out with head bent under a cap. Our meerkat-like sentry relaxed and glanced at her watch.

I had another sip of water and watched the traffic passing back and forth on the A-road which followed the horizon line. Mostly cars, HGVs, some tractors, as this was the edgelands, the dirty fringe between city and countryside — or rather, the agricultural land we dress up as countryside. Then the truck passed by, in the northbound direction, crossing my field of view from left to right like an apparition before disappearing behind the treeline.

People got to their feet. There was a minute of organising. Then its nose pushed out from around the corner, almost hesitantly.

As it drove up the track, the cargo was politely silent. It rolled to a heavy stop, and the man in the fleece walked up to speak to the driver.

We were given the nod, and a few of us stepped from the verge. It was a short approach — a couple of metres — and slightly downhill, so that when I reached the body of the truck, my eyeline was below the first fenestra, and I was forced to balance on my toes.

I had expected rolling eyes and foaming chops, but when I looked into the truck I was met with more of a benevolent curiosity. A big, pink face rose to meet mine. She had a little dirt dried in the space above her snout, and though she had no visible eyebrows, when she lifted her eyes, her brow furrowed questioningly, and I thought of my mother. Her large ears were spotted, though whether with dirt or in colouration I wasn't sure. They folded bashfully across her face like the bells of a wilted flower. Her neighbour had one ear turned inside out, giving him the baffled, comical look seen in dogs loping madly round the park, ears smacking with the beat of their bodies against the wind.

The first tipped the long tube of her face up to meet my hand, and pushed her snout against my fingers. She opened her mouth, and suckled a little, very softly. At the local sanctuary, I had seen these jaws crush a watermelon. We stayed like this for a few seconds, my fingers tugged against the ribbing of her palate. Her eyelashes were small and white.

Time was called. I stepped backwards out of the way, and the truck heaved through the gates, the barrier raised as if this were the entrance to a car park, pointing to the sky. I took off my hi-vis and walked back to my car. As I buckled up to drive home, the truck sailed past, empty, much lighter.

www.ingramcontent.com/pod-product-compliance
Lightning Source LLC
Chambersburg PA
CBHW061346040426
42444CB00011B/3121
* 9 7 8 1 9 1 3 6 4 2 5 6 3 *